Tut, Tut, Pup!

Written by Jeanne Willis
Illustrated by Sonia Esplugas

The duck pecks.
Peck, peck, peck.

The ram kicks.
Kick, kick, kick.

The rat rips.
Rip, rip, rip.

The pup tugs.
Tug, tug, tug.

No, Pup, no!

Go, Pup, go!

Mop it up.
Tut, tut, tut!